101
SCHOOL JOKES

Adirondack Central School
Boonville Middle Library

Make Me Laugh! 101 SCHOOL

by Sam Schultz / pictures by Joan Hanson

JOKES
guaranteed to keep you awake in class

Lerner Publications Company · Minneapolis

Library of Congress Cataloging in Publication Data

Schultz, Sam.
    101 school jokes.

    (Make me laugh)
    Summary: A collection of jokes and riddles about
school and education.
    1. Education—Anecdotes, facetiae, satire, etc.
2. Wit and humor, Juvenile. [1. Education—
Anecdotes, facetiae, satire, etc. 2. Jokes.
3. Riddles] I. Hanson, Joan, ill. II. Title.
III. Title: One hundred one school jokes. IV. Title:
One hundred and one school jokes. V. Series.
PN6231.S3S34   818'.5402   81-20912
ISBN 0-8225-0979-2   AACR2

Manufactured in the United States of America

2   3   4   5   6   7   8   9   10   91   90   89   88   87   86   85   84   83

Jack: What's the toughest thing for you in school?

Mack: Trying to whisper to the kid next to me without moving my lips.

First Student: How did you do with the test questions?

Second Student: I did fine with the questions. It's the answers I had trouble with!

Teacher: Why are you running?

Boy: I'm running to stop a fight.

Teacher: Between who?

Boy: Between me and the guy who's chasing me!

Teacher: In what battle did General Wolfe cry, "I die happy"?

Student: His last one.

Arnie: I wish I had been born a thousand years ago.

Les: Why?

Arnie: Just think of all the history I wouldn't have to study!

Q: What's worse than finding a worm in your apple?

A: Finding half a worm!

Billy: Why weren't you in school today?
Willy: I had a toothache so I went to the dentist.
Billy: Does your tooth still ache?
Willy: I don't know. The dentist kept it!

Daughter: Dad, can you write your name in the dark?

Dad: I think so.

Daughter: Great. Would you please turn off the lights and sign my report card?

Teacher: Sandy, you spelled that word perfectly. Do you read the dictionary?

Sandy: No, but I saw the movie.

Q: Where do we get milk?

A: From the supermarket!

Teacher: All these homework problems in math are wrong.

Student: Better not let my dad find out.

Teacher: Why not? Will he punish you?

Student: No. He told me math was his best subject!

Father: What happened in school today?
Betsy: My teacher made a mistake in arithmetic.
Father: Really? What kind of mistake?
Betsy: Well, yesterday she told us that two plus two makes four, and today she told us that three plus one makes four.

Q: Who knows the president of France?
A: The president's wife.

Sister: How have you been doing in school, Bobby?
Bobby: Well, I've been working hard to get ahead.
Sister: That's good. You could certainly use one.

Teacher: Why are the Middle Ages called the Dark Ages?
Student: Because there were so many knights.

Q: What's the definition of dogma?
A: A dogma is a puppy's mother.

Teacher: Joan, if I had six oranges in one hand and seven in the other, what would I have?
Joan: Very big hands!

Teacher: This is the fifth time this week I've had to punish you. What do you have to say for yourself?

Student: Thank *goodness* it's Friday!

Q: What's the capital of Alaska?

A: Juneau?

Q: Of course I do but I'm asking you!

Science Teacher: Who can tell me what an atom is?

Student: Isn't that the guy who went with Eve?

Student: I don't think I deserve a zero on this test.

Teacher: Neither do I. But it's the lowest grade I can give you.

Mother: Lois, why are you crying?
Lois: My teacher yelled at me for something I didn't do.
Mother: What was it you didn't do?
Lois: My homework!

Teacher: Will you two stop passing notes!
Student: We're not passing notes. We're playing cards!

Q: What's bacteria?
A: The rear entrance to the cafeteria.

Father: Arnie, your teacher told me you're at the bottom of the class.
Arnie: So what, Dad? We learn the same things at both ends.

Teacher: Children, open your geography books. Who can tell me where South America is?
Student: I know! It's on page 15.

Tom: I won't be coming to school tomorrow.
   I'll be home sick.
John: I didn't know you were sick.
Tom: I will be after my mom sees my report card!

Teacher: Donald, I hope I didn't see you looking at Andy's paper.

Donald: I hope you didn't either!

Grandma: Tell me what you did in school today.

Ted: We did Adzuptus.

Grandma: Really? How do you do that?

Ted: One and one adzuptu two, two and two adzuptu four.

Mother: I know my daughter talks a lot in class, but she *is* trying.

Teacher: She certainly is!

Teacher: How do you know the earth is round?

Student: Why are you asking me? I never said it was.

Teacher: Well, there's one good thing I can say about your son.

Father: Oh? What's that?

Teacher: With grades like his, he can't possibly be cheating!

Boy on Phone: Mom, they're starving us here at boarding school.

Mom: Oh dear! What are they feeding you?

Boy: Just breakfast, lunch, and dinner!

Q: Who knows what an echo is?

A: Could you repeat the question?

Mother: How do you like school, Cathy?

Cathy: Closed.

Teacher: Ernie, I thought I told you I never want
to see you walk into this classroom late again.
Ernie: I know, that's why I'm crawling in!

Teacher: If you have three chocolate bars and I ask you to give me one, how many will you have left?
Student: Three.

There once was a teacher named Bass
Who stood at the head of the class.
And he said with a smirk,
"Those who don't do homework
Get a party on me if they pass!"

Q: Where do dates grow?
A: On calendar trees.

Q: What's a barbarian?
A: That's the guy who cuts your hair in the library!

Teacher: I'd like to go just one day without having to make you stay after school!
Student: OK, permission granted.

Mother: Johnny, I hope you're not talking in class anymore since your teacher sent me that note.

Johnny: Nope. Not any more, but not any less, either!

Teacher: A,B,C,D,E,F,G. What comes after G?

Student: Whiz.

Chris: Mom, could you help me with my math homework?

Mom: No, Chris, it wouldn't be right.

Chris: That's okay, as long as you give it a try!

Teacher: Jerry, don't you have something to tell me?

Jerry: No, ma'am.

Teacher: Didn't you miss school yesterday?

Jerry: Not a bit. I had a ball!

Teacher: Jackie, you've been late to school every day since school began. What's the reason?

Jackie: I can't help it. The sign on the street says, "School, go slow."

Teacher: When you think of Greece, what's the
first thing that comes to your mind?
Student: French fries.

Teacher: Donny, let's pretend you're a big game hunter, and you suddenly come across an alligator, a lion, and a rhinocerous. Which one would you get fur from?

Donny: I'd get as fur from all of them as I could get.

Q: Where was the Declaration of Independence signed?

A: At the bottom.

A teacher asked her class to make a list of the nine greatest living Americans.

Teacher: Are you finished with your list yet, Pete?

Pete: Not yet. I still have to think of a third baseman.

Q: Did you hear about the little boy who runs home every day after school?

A: He's trying to make the *Guiness Book of World Records* for the kid with the most home runs!

It was the first day of school after Christmas vacation.

Mother: Mary, explain why you got a 60 on this math test!

Mary: Oh, our teacher always marks things down after Christmas.

Jerry: I'm not going to school today, Mom. Nobody there likes me.

Mother: That's nonsense, Jerry. Besides, you have to go to school today. You're the principal!

Manny: My boy scout troop had to carry an old
   lady across the street yesterday.
Teacher: Why did you have to carry her?
Manny: Because she didn't want to go!

Teacher: Harvey, you didn't wash your face this
   morning, did you? I can see you had eggs for
   breakfast.
Harvey: No I didn't, teacher. I had cereal.
   I had eggs yesterday!

Q: Who won at Bull Run?
A: I don't know. Was the score in the papers?

Teacher: Susie, you don't seem to be paying any attention to me. Are you having trouble hearing?
Susie: No, I'm having trouble listening!

Q: How many months have 28 days?
A: All of them.

School would really be okay
If we had an extra holiday.
Or two, or three, or maybe ten.
School might not be so awful then.
Another thing that would be cool
Is having Friday off from school!

Larry: My mother's going to night school.
Teacher: Really? Why?
Larry: I don't know. I guess she wants to learn to read in the dark!

Billy's Mother: Billy told me he got 100 on his tests yesterday!
Billy's Teacher: He did. 50 in spelling and 50 in arithmetic.

A third-grade class went to the museum. On a glass case with a mummy in it, there was a sign that said, "400 B.C."
Teacher: Who can tell the class what the sign means?
Student: That's the license number of the car that hit him!

Alice: Mom, my teacher told me not to take any more baths!

Mother: Are you sure that's what she said?

Alice: Well, she told me to stay out of hot water or she'd keep me after school!

Teacher: Teddy, you come right up here and give me what you've got in your mouth.

Teddy: I don't think you'd want it, teacher. It's a toothache!

The teacher had just handed out report cards.

Billy: Miss Jones, I don't want to scare you or anything, but my dad told me that if I don't take home a good report card, somebody's going to get spanked!

Teacher: Dennis, what should I do about you? You never get to school on time.

Dennis: Just don't wait, teacher. Go ahead and start without me.

Teacher: Mary, tell your classmates what you share with your parents.

Mary: My homework.

Q: Who knows something about Buddha?

A: That's what we used before my mother switched to margarine.

Father: How was school today?
Son: It wouldn't be so bad if my teacher wasn't so dumb.
Father: What do you mean?
Son: All she does all day long is ask us silly questions.

Teacher: Johnny, if you take 2 from 5, and 2 from 6, what's the difference?
Johnny: I know what you mean. It doesn't make any difference to me, either.

Jimmy: My brother goes to college.
Teacher: Really? What does he take?
Jimmy: Anything Mom and Pop will give him.

Teacher: I wish you'd pay a little attention to me, Sally.
Sally: I am, teacher. As little as possible!

Father: What does this "F" on your report card mean?

Student: "Fantastic!"

Q: How would you find the English Channel?
A: By turning the dial on the television set.

Mother: What did you learn in school today?
Child: My teacher taught us writing.
Mother: What did you write?
Child: I don't know. She hasn't taught us reading yet.

Teacher: Ronnie, why is it so difficult for you to learn how to spell?
Ronnie: Because you keep changing the words!

Teacher: Timmy, if you were standing in California, which would be farthest away, New York City or the moon?
Timmy: New York City.
Teacher: What makes you say that?
Timmy: I can see the moon, but I can't see New York City!

Q: How do you spell Mississippi?
A: The river or the state?

Betsy: Mom, you won't have to buy me any new school books next year.
Mom: That's good news. Why not?
Betsy: Because my teacher didn't pass me.

Teacher: Did your father help you with these arithmetic problems?
Student: No, teacher. I got them wrong all by myself.

Father: (Sternly) I received a note from your teacher today, Dickie.
Dickie: That's okay, Pop. I won't tell Mom.

Teacher: Ronald told me you threw a rock
through my classroom window.
Albert: It's not my fault, it's Ronald's fault.
Teacher: Why is it Ronald's fault?
Albert: When I threw the rock at him,
he ducked!

Teacher: George, this story you turned in, called "Our Cat," is exactly the same as your brother's.

George: Well, what did you expect? It's the same cat.

Teacher: Tommy, if you could save a dollar a week for a whole year, what would you have?

Tommy: I'd have a new bike!

Teacher: William, did Ellen help you with these arithmetic problems?

William: No, ma'am.

Teacher: Are you sure?

William: Honest, she didn't help me. She did them all herself.

Q: Do you know Lincoln's Gettysburg Address?

A: I thought he lived in the White House.

Teacher: Marty, why haven't you returned your report card?

Marty: Because you gave me two A's. My parents are still showing it to all the relatives!

Mother: Why did you get such a low grade on your test today, Barry?

Barry: The kid who sits next to me was absent.

Johnny: Teacher, I ain't got a pencil.

Teacher: Johnny, I *haven't* got a pencil.

Johnny: That makes two of us.

Bus Driver: Do you want to go to Fifth Street School?

Little Girl: No. I have to.

Q: What's the difference between a school teacher and a train engineer?

A: A school teacher trains the mind, and a train engineer minds the train.

Father: How do you like your new school, Rodney?

Rodney: I don't think I'm going to like it, Dad. It's haunted.

Father: That's silly. Who told you that?

Rodney: The teacher. He keeps talking about the school spirit.

Voice on Phone: Is this the principal?
Principal: Yes.
Voice on Phone: Jenny Smith is too sick to come
   to school today.
Principal: Who's calling, please?
Voice on Phone: This is my mother.

Q: What does your father do?
A: He works with the stars.
Q: Is he in the movie business?
A: No, he's an astronomer.

Q: What do you call a horse doctor?
A: A doctor with a sore throat.

Teacher: What important change came about
   due to the invention of the automobile?
Student: It stopped horse stealing.

Q: What did George Washington, Abraham
   Lincoln, and Christopher Columbus have in
   common?
A: They were all born on holidays.

Teacher: What did Benjamin Franklin say when he discovered electricity?
Student: "Ouch!"

Johnny: Mom, my teacher said my penmanship is awful.
Mom: Then why don't you practice and make it better?
Johnny: No. Then she'll figure out I can't spell!

Q: When did Columbus discover America?
A: On Columbus Day.

Teacher: What do you expect to be when you get out of school?
Student: A very old man!

ABOUT THE AUTHOR

SAM SCHULTZ began telling jokes to children when his own were very young, and today he likes to think up new jokes while jogging on the beach near his home in Santa Monica, California. Mr. Schultz has been a writer for several advertising agencies, and now he writes scripts for television shows and children's films.

ABOUT THE ARTIST

JOAN HANSON lives with her husband and two sons in Afton, Minnesota, a tiny village on the St. Croix River. Her distinctive, deliberately whimsical pen-and-ink drawings have illustrated 30 children's books. Ms. Hanson is also an accomplished weaver, and while that art form takes up most of her time, she enjoys sketching and finds it a refreshing change from her weaving.

Make Me Laugh!